Routes of Cross-Cultural Exchange

The Northwest Passage

Rachel Keranen

Cavendish Square
New York

Published in 2018 by Cavendish Square Publishing, LLC
243 5th Avenue, Suite 136, New York, NY 10016

First Edition

CPSIA Compliance Information: Batch #CS17CSQ

Library of Congress Cataloging-in-Publication Data

Names: Keranen, Rachel, author.
Title: The Northwest Passage / Rachel Keranen.
Description: New York : Cavendish Square Publishing, [2018] | Series: Routes of cross-cultural exchange | Includes bibliographical references and index.
Identifiers: LCCN 2017000085 (print) | LCCN 2017001592 (ebook) | ISBN 9781502626950 (library bound) | ISBN 9781502626899 (E-book)
Subjects: LCSH: Northwest Passage--History--Juvenile literature. | Northwest Passage--Discovery and exploration--Juvenile literature. | Trade routes--History--Juvenile literature.
Classification: LCC G640 .K47 2018 (print) | LCC G640 (ebook) | DDC 910.9163/27--dc23
LC record available at https://lccn.loc.gov/2017000085

Editorial Director: David McNamara
Editor: Caitlyn Miller
Copy Editor: Michele Suchomel-Casey
Associate Art Director: Amy Greenan
Designer: Jessica Nevins
Production Coordinator: Karol Szymczuk
Photo Research: J8 Media

The photographs in this book are used by permission and through the courtesy of: Cover, p. 80 Paul Nicklen/National Geographic/Getty Images; p. 5 City Escapes Nature Photo/Shutterstock.com; p. 8 Tropical studio/Shutterstock.com; p. 10 Pingebat/iStock/Thinkstock; p. 13 Maxiphoto/iStock; p. 15 Gordon Wiltsie/National Geographic/Getty Images; p. 18 gallimaufry/Shutterstock.com; p. 23 ugljesa/Shutterstock.com; p. 26 pavalena/Shutterstock.com; p. 33 Rainer Lesniewski/Shutterstock.com; p. 34 Sovfoto/Universal Images Group/Getty Images; p. 40 Venus Angel/Shutterstock.com; p. 44 Universal History Archive/Universal Images Group/Getty Images; p. 48 Peter Horree/Alamy Stock Photo; p. 51 Hulton Archive/Getty Images; p. 54 duncan1890/iStock; p. 57 B Christopher/Alamy Stock Photo; p. 60 RyersonClark/iStock; p. 65 Antonioptg/Wikimedia Commons/File:UNCLOS-en.png/CC BY-SA 4.0; p. 66 200mm/iStock; p. 74 NASA/Wikimedia Commons/File:Northwest Passage 09-08-13.jpg/CC PD; p. 77 ValentinaKru/Shutterstock.com; p. 82 RENAULT Philippe/hemis.fr/Getty Images.

Printed in the United States of America

Table of Contents

Introduction

Crossing the Arctic

For centuries, a route from the Atlantic Ocean to the Pacific Ocean via the Arctic fascinated and eluded European merchants and explorers.

When the Middle Ages ended in Europe and the Age of Discovery began, European explorers set sail across the globe. They found a wealth of treasure in the East Indies, India, China, and Japan, including spices, textiles, incense, ceramics, and more. Demand for goods from the Far East soared in Europe, especially for spices such as nutmeg, cloves, and black pepper.

To get to the Far East, navigators found long sea routes south around Africa and South America. The Portuguese and Spanish were the first to find and control these routes, followed by the Dutch. By the time the English and French began to explore in earnest, the known sea routes to Asia were already controlled by rival nations. The East Indies themselves were controlled primarily by the Dutch. England and France would need to find new routes—and ideally new islands—to share in the luxuries of the Far East.

Baffin Bay is bordered by Greenland (the Greenlandic village of Uummannaq is shown here) and Baffin Island.

The only potential new routes were to the north through the Arctic Ocean. At this time in history, little was known about the far north other than that it was very cold and filled with ice. Nevertheless, many in England believed that if explorers headed north, they would find a new and shorter route to the Pacific Ocean and the Far East. Their desire for spices and treasure gave them more optimism than was warranted.

England dominated the initial search for an Arctic sea route. After a deathly failed attempt to find a northeast passage over Russia, the northern quest focused primarily on finding a northwest passage over North America.

In the 1570s, the English navigator Martin Frobisher made the first three voyages to the Arctic northwest. Frobisher's voyages turned out to be complete failures from both an economic and an exploratory standpoint.

Over the next three hundred years, England sent voyage after voyage to the Arctic to probe for a passage to the Pacific. Explorers such as Henry Hudson scoured Hudson Bay looking for a strait to the northwest. Other explorers like William Baffin sailed through the Davis Strait and Baffin Bay to look for a far northerly route. Still others attempted to follow the Canadian northern coastline, certain that doing so would eventually lead them to the Pacific Ocean.

In all expeditions, the dangers of the Arctic waterways proved challenging and often fatal. The long voyages ventured into a region with no plant life most of the year. The lack of plants meant that crews suffered from crippling malnutrition. The climate was cold and windy, causing frostbite and hypothermia. Floating ice, constant fog, and strong winds made navigation range from difficult to impossible. In many cases, ships were savagely battered by ice.

In the end, success came in a form very different than that of the English expeditions. In the early 1900s, the Norwegian explorer Roald Amundsen bought a small boat with an engine and hired six crewmen. His expedition spent over a year in the Arctic taking scientific observations before continuing west and completing the Northwest Passage.

In 1940–1942, another Norwegian serving in the Royal Canadian Mounted Police named Henry Larsen became the first to transit the Northwest Passage from west to east. In 1944, Larsen became the first to transit the Northwest Passage in a single season. Larsen used different routes in his journeys.

(Today, there are as many as seven Northwest Passage routes because different routes are recognized by different people.)

Since those first successful passages in the early twentieth century, the Northwest Passage has remained more of a potential trade route than one that has come into wide use. Though it is possible to get through the Northwest Passage, it is still very dangerous. Arctic sea ice is melting at rapid rates due to climate change, but **ice floes** and icebergs still present significant navigational challenges. The lack of infrastructure, such as seaports for safe harbor and ice-breaking vessels that can aid ships passing through, makes safety an even bigger issue.

As climate change continues to melt the ice in the Arctic, the Northwest Passage will become more of a viable (possible) trade route. The global economy has changed significantly since the 1500s, and Great Britain is no longer the primary nation interested in the trade route. Countries such as China, Canada, and the United States are preparing for the possibility of a usable Northwest Passage.

It is still uncertain what the future of the Northwest Passage will look like and how much it will ever be used for trade. Nevertheless, the nations most likely to benefit from it are preparing for the logistics and infrastructure necessary to support using the trade route.

Chapter 1

Trade Before the Northwest Passage

Explorers and governments first began seeking a northwest passage because of global trade conditions. During a period lasting roughly from the fifteenth century to the eighteenth century, European nations were hungry for prized goods from the Far East, especially the East Indies. Therefore, Europeans were eager to find quick, easy routes to Asia. The first established routes went south of South America and Africa.

The East Indies

The East Indies (also called the Indies or the Spice Islands) are the islands that extend along the equator for more than 3,800 miles (6,115.5 kilometers) between the Asian mainland and Australia.

Opposite: *Clove trees are evergreens indigenous to Indonesia. Cloves are used in cooking and baking, such as in pumpkin pie.*

Indonesia is made up of more than seventeen thousand islands and has the world's fourth largest population.

There are various interpretations of the boundaries of the East Indies. In the most common use of the term, the East Indies are the islands that now make up Indonesia, including Borneo, Java, the Moluccas, and New Guinea.

The Indonesian **archipelago** (cluster of islands) is made up of mountainous islands with dense rain forests. The islands are home to plants such as the *Myristica fragrans*, or common nutmeg tree. Another valuable plant is the *Piper nigrum* vine, which produces black peppercorns. These types of plants are not found in Europe, and they created the powerful, enormous global spice trade. (Spices are also found in places near the East Indies like the Indian subcontinent.)

The spice trade first arrived in the Middle East at least four thousand years ago, making southern Arabia a center for the spice trade. The Romans sailed from Egypt (in northeastern Africa) to India in the beginning of the first millennium BCE. They traded with India for several centuries. However, the Arabian spice trade dominated until the Middle Ages. During the Middle Ages, Venice established a monopoly on trade with the Middle East. This left Venetians free to raise the price of spices for buyers in northern and western Europe.

Portuguese Maritime Trade Routes to Asia

In the fifteenth century, European explorers began to build ships and sail to Asia. They were motivated to explore in order to break the Venetian monopoly on the spice trade. This period of time is known as the European Age of Discovery. The maritime routes explorers developed expanded the network of the Silk Road significantly.

In a voyage spanning 1497 to 1499, the Portuguese explorer Vasco da Gama became the first European to reach India via sea. Da Gama's route headed south of Europe from Lisbon, went south around Africa and the Cape of Good Hope, and back north to India. The route was long and difficult. But it was free of competition.

The Silk Road

The network of trade routes stretching between China and the Mediterranean is known as the Silk Road. These routes consisted of land and maritime routes that shifted over time as the politics and geography of the region shifted. Altogether, the network of routes was in use through the Middle Ages and into the nineteenth century.

In addition to silk, for which the roads earned their name, textiles, spices, grains, tools, metals, art, precious stones, and much more were traded. Spices tended to be traded via the sea-based routes.

The Silk Road was also responsible for significant exchange of art, culture, science, technology, religion, and more. Those who traveled the Silk Road impacted and were impacted by the cultures they visited. They brought back those influences to their home cities. Papermaking, for example, spread through the Silk Road, as did the development of the printing press.

While its name is famous today, the term "the Silk Road" was coined by the German geographer and geologist Baron Ferdinand von Richthofen in the nineteenth century. Baron von Richthofen traveled extensively through China to do field work and traveled along portions of the Silk Road. In the original German, the name he gave the routes was Seidenstraße.

In 2016, China announced a plan to help develop countries along the former Silk Road by investing in infrastructure such as new roads, railways, and pipelines. By modernizing and increasing the infrastructure in foreign countries, China will increase the market for its goods and new investment opportunities for Chinese companies.

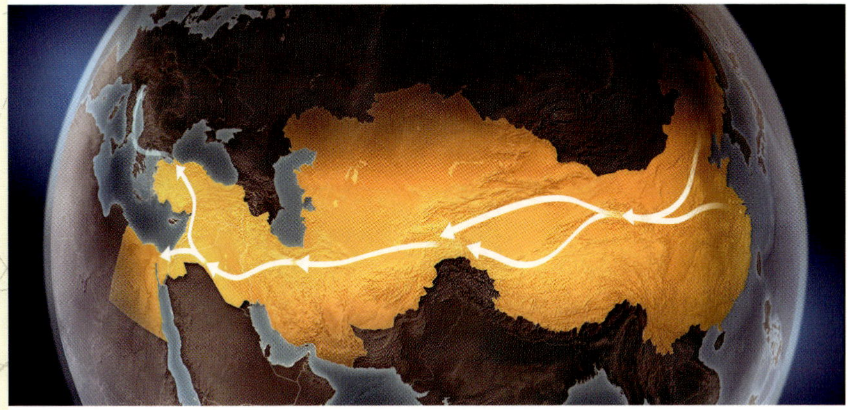

The Silk Road's land routes linked the Far East and central Asia with Mesopotamia and the Mediterranean.

Two years later, a Portuguese navigator named Pedro Álvares Cabral led the first successful maritime expedition from Europe to Asia. (Cabral is also credited with discovering Brazil.) Going forward, Portugal controlled the African sea route and dominated the spice trade throughout the sixteenth century. Meanwhile, Spain gained control of the sea routes around the Americas.

The Dutch Replace the Portuguese

Dutch expeditions sailed for the Spice Islands in 1595 and 1598. Sailors brought back cloves, mace, nutmeg, and black pepper. These trips also laid the foundation for the Dutch East India Company, formed in 1602. As the Dutch gained control, Portuguese influence waned. By the nineteenth century, the Dutch were the major force colonizing and profiting from the East Indies. The English were strong presences in India and Ceylon (today called Sri Lanka), too.

By the time the English and the French began looking for trade routes to the Far East, the known routes were already flooded with competitors. Both the English and the French sought alternative ways to get to Asia through North America, directly leading to the centuries-long hunt for the Northwest Passage.

Native North American Trade Routes

Before Europeans ever set foot on the shores of North America, there were native trade routes stretching across Canada and Alaska.

The Inuit

The **Inuit**, or the native people of northern Canada, Alaska, and Greenland, have lived in North America for about a thousand years. The Inuit have also been called Eskimos. This name might have derived from the French word *esquimaux*, or "one who nets snowshoes." Today, however, the word "Eskimo" is considered to be a **pejorative** (negative). "Inuit" is the preferred term.

The Inuit have a unique culture well adapted to the cold, harsh environment they inhabit. Early Inuit wore clothing made out of skins from animals, including caribou, seals, and arctic foxes. They traveled using dogsleds and light boats such as kayaks, and they hunted caribou, sea mammals, and fish. In the summers, the Inuit built tents made from animal skins. In the winters, they built houses called igloos made of blocks of snow.

Trees are a scarce commodity in the Arctic (the word "tundra" comes from the Finnish word *tunturi*,

This hunter's harpoon has a rope so he can easily retrieve the weapon after he has thrown it after his prey.

which means "treeless plain"). Therefore, the Inuit used animal skins, hides, oil, and bones for almost all of their tools and boats. Metal was also a rare commodity, although there was some copper in the central Arctic. Iron was the most valued resource, but the only natural source of iron in the Inuit lands was from meteors. Otherwise, iron had to be traded for with European whalers or Russians, or gathered from the ruins and remnants of European expeditions.

The Inuit have an oral history tradition, which means that history and knowledge are passed on from generation to generation with remarkable accuracy through storytelling. Knowledge of Inuit trade routes was passed on in this manner.

A native trade network extended from the Bering Strait to the region of the Coppermine Inuit near Coronation Gulf, east to the Hudson Bay coast, and beyond to Baffin Island and to northwestern Greenland. The routes consisted of walking trails, sled routes, and open water routes instead of easily identifiable, permanent trails. The routes changed based on the season. The various routes enabled the Inuit to take paths that led them near animals for hunting and survival.

There were two primary routes. One, a winter route, stretched across southern Victoria Island to Banks Island where Kangiryuarmiut Inuit were met by Mackenzie Inuit. The Mackenzie Inuit crossed to Banks Island over sea ice from Cape Parry. The other route stretched along the southern coast of Amundsen Gulf.

Along these routes, the Inuit traded lamps and pots of **soapstone** (a soft rock) manufactured by the Coppermine Inuit in the central Arctic with their western neighbors. These items were traded as far west as the Bering Strait and into Siberia in Russia. In return, the Inuit in the western Arctic received Russian metals and metal goods, especially the highly valuable Russian iron knives.

There was also some trade of Alaskan furs for Russian metal goods across the Bering Strait as early as 1742. By the 1780s, these metal goods had already moved across the native trade routes to the Mackenzie Delta area, along with reports of white men in large canoes.

The Russian trade expanded to include tobacco and beads as well as Siberian spotted reindeer goods in return for Alaskan furs, oil, ivory, and carved wooden implements.

There was a large network of trade routes across the Arctic by the time the British began searching for a northwest trade route to Asia. However, there was little European knowledge of the region they hoped to navigate.

Latitude and Longitude

In the next chapter, we'll discuss the search for the Northwest Passage. When describing the various expeditions and accomplishments, we'll describe geographic locations in terms of latitude and longitude.

Latitude describes the distance a point is north or south of Earth's equator. There are 90 degrees of latitude north and south of the equator, and each degree is composed of 60 minutes. Each minute is composed of 60 seconds, but in this book we'll round to the closest degree and minute. New York City, for example, is at 40 degrees and 43 minutes north, or 40°43'N.

Longitude describes the distance a point is east or west from the **meridian** at Greenwich, England, which is called the Prime Meridian. (A meridian is an imaginary continuous line that connects the North Pole and South Pole.) There are 180 degrees of longitude east and west of the Prime Meridian. New York City, for example, is at 73 degrees and 56 minutes west, or 73°56'W.

Polus 90 Arcticus
AMERICA SIVE INDIA NOVA
Anno Dñi 1492 à Christophoro Colombo nomine Regis Castellę primum detecta.
Circulus Arcticus
Anian regnum
Bergi regio
Quiuira reg.
Tolm reg.
Chilaga
Hochelaga
Saguenay
Canada
Norombega
Florida
Golfo Mexicano
Nova Francia
Estotilant
Groenlant
Mare dulce
Circulus Aequinoctialis
Tropicus Capricorni
Castilia del Oro
Peru
Chili
Paraguai
Archipelago minore
Estrecho de Magellanes
Terra del fuego
TERRA AUSTRALIS.
Circulus Antarcticus
Patagones
La Bermuda
Guanahani insula

Chapter 2

Foundations and Explorations

For much of Western history, there was little knowledge of the land and sea above 65°N other than that the region was icy and bitterly cold. The Vikings had explored Iceland, Greenland, and even western Canada, but western Europeans knew little of their discoveries.

During the 1500s, maps of the Arctic were left vague. They were labeled with terms such as "Mare glaciale" or "Congelatum" (frozen sea) and were wildly inaccurate. The geography of the northern coast of North America was entirely unknown.

European Desire for a Northwest Passage

Eager to capitalize on the wealth that their European rivals were bringing home from their conquests, the

Opposite: *This 1587 map by Gerald Mercator shows a then-common belief that the Arctic was composed of four islands surrounding a magnetic black rock.*

French were the first to search for a more northern route to Asia.

In 1524, Giovanni da Verrazano led a French expedition to North America and sailed from South Carolina to Maine in a search for a route to the Pacific. He discovered New York Harbor and Narragansett Bay but no break in the coastline. A decade later, Jacques Cartier explored the Canadian coastline in 1534 and the St. Lawrence River in 1535, claiming the land he found for King Francis I of France.

By 1604, French explorers had established the first European settlements north of Florida in present-day Maine and Nova Scotia. The French Empire in Canada, fueled by the fur trade, had begun. Meanwhile, the English had picked up the search for a northwest passage.

The English first tried to find a northeast passage to Asia by sailing along Russia's north coast. The ill-fated expedition, led by Sir Hugh Willoughby and Richard Chancellor in 1553, ended with all sixty-three of Willoughby's men dead. Chancellor's ship made it only as far as the White Sea north of Moscow.

The northeast passage had proved deadly, and Russia was controlled by the tsar. In comparison, the Northwest Passage was untested by the English and free of monarchies. In 1576, the first English ships set sail to find the hoped-for passage.

Because the search spanned so much time with the promise of great financial reward and historical acclaim, there were many more expeditions than we can cover in this book. This chapter includes several of the most notable, especially heroic, or tragic expeditions.

Explorers who made contributions to the search but are not detailed in this book include: Luke Foxe, Thomas James, Sir John Ross, Frederick William Beechey, Sir George Back, and Sir Alexander MacKenzie. Their stories are worth reading.

Dangers of the Arctic

As we'll see in the expeditions that follow, Arctic explorers faced many obstacles. The most challenging and universal obstacles were the freezing temperatures, crushing ice floes (sheets of floating ice), and disease.

Summer in the Arctic is mild and very short. James Bay in the Hudson Bay, for example, is at the same latitude as London. However, James Bay is not navigable until June due to ice.

Winter begins in September and fades into complete darkness for months with average low temperatures around -35° Fahrenheit (-37° Celsius). The English explorers were usually outfitted in woolen clothing, which neither blocked wind nor wicked away sweat.

Arctic sea ice can be meters deep, and it shifts quickly. A clear channel can open and close in the matter of an hour. Wind can drive ice floes into a channel and block it with thick ice for years. The unluckiest of explorers discovered this firsthand. That same ice can tear into boats and damage or sink them. Icebergs as tall as 300 feet (91.4 meters) drift south through the region and threaten to sink ships. Fog is common and obscures navigators' ability to see the horizon, making it difficult to chart a course or spot passage openings.

Scurvy was another major, deadly challenge that plagued voyages during the search for the Northwest Passage. The disease sets in after about three months without sufficient vitamin C from plants such as strawberries, brussels sprouts, and oranges. Symptoms include constant fatigue, irritation, limb pain, dark patches of skin, swollen gums, loose teeth, and bleeding inside the joints and muscles.

On some voyages, especially those forced to spend more years in the Arctic than expected, food ran short, causing extreme hunger and even starvation.

Early English Expeditions

The first English expedition to cross the Atlantic in search of Asia was led by John Cabot in 1497. Historians don't know precisely where Cabot landed, but it was somewhere on the eastern coast of Canada. Cabot believed he had reached Asia and headed back to England.

It was soon clear that the North American continent was not Asia but a landmass between Europe and Asia. In the 1570s, the English began looking for a northwest passage above North America in earnest, starting a search that continued for centuries.

Frobisher's Voyages

In 1576, Sir Martin Frobisher made it as far as Labrador (the northeastern portion of Canada's mainland) and Baffin Island (an island located between Greenland and Canada). One of his three ships, a very small **pinnace**, sank in the Davis Strait. (A pinnace is a small boat designed to accompany a larger vessel. It is used to communicate between ships or perform other, more nimble tasks.) Another ship, the *Michael*, turned home. The third ship, the *Gabriel*, continued alone.

The Arctic consists primarily of salt water and sea ice but also contains freshwater glaciers and icebergs.

Frobisher discovered Frobisher's Straits (actually an inlet in Baffin Island, now known as Frobisher's Bay). He also came across Inuit living on Baffin Island. The Inuit had dark hair, tan skin, and other characteristics that led Frobisher to believe that the Inuit were actually Asian.

Frobisher's crew and the Inuit exchanged gifts. But the encounter ended on a dark note when five men sailed in a boat with an Inuit who volunteered to act as a guide. The men were never seen again. It is not known whether the men were kidnapped or chose to live with the Inuit for the winter before dying in an attempt to sail home the next year. As revenge, Frobisher took an **Inuk** (the singular form of Inuit) captive and turned back for England.

While sailing, a small boat from the *Gabriel* landed on a small island to the southeast of Baffin Island. Here, the group picked up a lump of black rock that they thought might be useful as fuel. When they returned to England, the black rock was analyzed and determined to contain gold.

Frobisher commanded another voyage in 1577 with a focus on bringing back gold ore rather than further exploring "Frobisher's Strait." He went again in 1578. This time he had fifteen ships in order to bring back more ore.

The crew returned with 1,250 pounds (566.9 kilograms) of ore but new tests showed that their cargo was useless. They had been mining and transporting iron pyrite, more commonly known as fool's gold.

Davis Heads North

Frobisher's failure did not quench England's thirst for a northwest passage to Asia. In June 1585, John Davis set sail toward Greenland with two ships. In July, Davis and his crew landed on the western coast of Greenland, where they were met by Inuit. Davis traded for local clothing and took off again, sailing northwest into Cumberland Sound before turning back.

Davis returned to the Arctic in 1586 and spent several weeks on islands near Greenland where he created an Inuit-to-English vocabulary. Tensions flared when iron items disappeared from Davis's ships, which led to skirmishes between the English and the Inuit.

One of Davis's ships arrived back in England with a load of sealskins, but the trip made no significant discoveries. He sailed again in 1587, heading through Davis Strait and into Baffin Bay, the opening to the Northwest Passage. Davis didn't realize the significance of where he was, but he did make it as far as 72°12'N, farther north than any European vessel had ever been.

Seventeenth-Century Explorations

The seventeenth century brought about further charting of the bays, straits, and coasts of the region, as well as tragedy.

Hudson Bay Discovered

Henry Hudson first looked for a northwest passage in 1609 when he sailed from Amsterdam on a contract with the Dutch East India Company. His mission was to look for a northeast passage and return to Amsterdam if he was unsuccessful. When weather forced him to turn back, however, Hudson headed west to find a passage rumored to exist at either 62°N or 40°N.

Hudson investigated the potential of a passage at 40°N and ended up sailing into the Hudson River. Realizing it was just a river, Hudson headed back to Europe. He docked in England, where the English government ordered Hudson and his crew to stop undergoing explorations for other countries.

In 1610, Hudson left England in pursuit of a potential passage at 60°N. His crew made it to the Hudson Strait, where ice pounded the ships and made passage very difficult, and into the Hudson Bay. Hudson was certain that they were on the Pacific side

Local ice builds up in Hudson Bay in winter, and pack ice drifts in from the basin to the north.

of North America, and he pushed forward. The crew was frozen in and became the first crew to spend an Arctic winter in pursuit of the Northwest Passage.

The winter was difficult, and the crew was afflicted by hunger and scurvy. Tensions rose as the crew believed Hudson was hoarding food for himself and his favorite crew members. When they left in June of 1611, the crew suspected that Hudson intended to keep looking for a northwest passage instead of going home.

The crew seized Hudson, tied him up, and put him in a small boat along with his son and six sick men from the ship. The carpenter of the ship stood up to the mutineers and joined Hudson and the others in the boat.

Hudson and his companions were set adrift and left to die, which they certainly did by the following winter. The ship sailed for London, but the ringleaders of the mutiny never made it back to England. They were killed in a fight with the Inuit en route home.

While Hudson was not a successful leader, he was a brave commander. He undertook four dangerous voyages in total, sustained his crew and ships through an unprecedented Arctic winter, and laid the foundation for Dutch colonization of the Hudson River and English colonization of Canada. (The Dutch controlled the Hudson River from 1609 until 1664, in which time they established the outpost of New Amsterdam, today known as New York City.)

Eighteenth-Century Expeditions

After unsuccessful attempts to find the passage by William Baffin in 1615 and 1616 and by Captain Thomas James and Captain Luke Foxe in 1631, English expeditions halted for about a century.

In 1745, the British Parliament issued a £20,000 reward for the discovery of a northwest passage. The act inspired many English to seek the route. In the 1760s and 1770s, Samuel Hearne completed three overland journeys west of Hudson Bay. His expedition showed that there was no northwest passage through the Hudson Bay.

In 1776, Captain James Cook approached the search from the Pacific Ocean instead of the Atlantic. Cook's crew sailed up the west coast of North America as far north as 70°N on August 17, 1778, before being halted by ice. This was a disappointment as other ships had sailed farther north in previous years.

It also highlights just how brief the navigable season in the Arctic is. For ten months of the year, the ice pack blocks passage between the Bering Strait and Point Barrow. For just a brief time in July and August a passage opens. Cook had arrived north too late to make much progress.

The British Parliament revised the promised reward to encourage even incremental progress. In 1777, the Discovery of North-West Passage Act was amended to give £5,000 for reaching 89°N. There was a £5,000 reward for sailing west of 100°W above the **Arctic Circle** (the region of the globe above 66°33'N). Finally, £1,000 awaited anyone who reached 83°N.

Nineteenth-Century Expeditions

In 1819, one of the most successful explorers in the search for the Northwest Passage captained a voyage to Lancaster Sound. William Parry planned to winter in the Arctic, and he brought lemon juice, sauerkraut, vinegar, and other vitamin C–rich foods to prevent scurvy in his crew. He planned classes as well as entertainment to get them through the hard winters.

Parry made it as far west as 113°46'W and won the £5,000 award for reaching that longitude above the Arctic Circle. He also explored 1,000 miles (1,609.3 km) of previously uncharted coastline.

Parry made several subsequent voyages, but neither Parry nor any other ship could make it farther west for many decades. The open ice conditions of 1819 were extremely rare.

In the 1820s, John Franklin led explorations of the North American northern coastline on foot and via canoe in 1819–1822 and 1825–1827. His goals were to supplement knowledge of the region gained at sea with information from land, to chart sea and ice conditions, and to find the southern shore of the Northwest Passage.

The first land voyage was disastrous. Franklin's men ate their spare boots to survive the winter. Eleven of twenty died, with rumors of cannibalism. The second was more successful, though. Altogether, Franklin's land expeditions mapped over 1,878 miles (3,022.3 km) of previously uncharted coastline.

In 1845, an aging Franklin (now Sir John Franklin) led an expedition of two ships, the HMS *Erebus* and the HMS *Terror*, and 128 men into the Northwest Passage. Both ships disappeared. This eventually sparked a massive years-long search for Franklin, his crew, and their ships.

Over centuries, searchers found remnants from the expedition and a single piece of paper with notes from 1847 and 1848. After spending a rather standard Arctic winter on Beechey Island, the ships had been frozen in for two winters at King William Island. John Franklin died, and the surviving officers and crew headed south on foot.

Oral history from the Inuit continued the narrative and told of starving, freezing white men. Some returned to the ships in hopes of rescue. Some resorted to cannibalism to survive but still died. Others continued walking south, dying one by one of scurvy, starvation, and cold.

The search for Franklin and his men helped fill in the knowledge gaps of the Arctic Archipelago. One searcher, Robert McClure, approached the passage from the Bering Strait in the west in 1850. McClure's ship became frozen in for two winters. While his ship was locked in the ice, McClure continued east on sledge and found a rescue ship. In doing so, McClure made the first complete transit of the Northwest Passage, though not the first complete voyage by boat. He and his crew received £10,000 from the British Parliament for their success.

The HMS *Erebus* was finally found in 2014, and the HMS *Terror* in 2016, both sunk off the coast of King William Island.

Success at Last

For centuries, the English had led the search for a northwest passage. In the end, however, it was a Norwegian expedition led by Roald Amundsen that made it through the Arctic.

Amundsen had read Franklin's journals and long dreamed of searching for the Northwest Passage. In 1900, Amundsen bought a small, sturdy fishing ship, which he had reinforced with iron and equipped with a thirteen-horsepower diesel engine that powered an iron propeller. Boat propellers were a recent invention, having first appeared in the early 1800s. He called the vessel the *Gjøa*.

Though the boat was small, Amundsen was able to pack enough food for five years for his six-man crew. His small crew was an intentional deviation from the past. To Amundsen, it meant every man understood the crucial role he played and was fully engaged.

Amundsen read all of the published accounts of previous Northwest Passage expeditions to form his route. He decided to sail through the straits between the Canadian mainland and the southern islands of the archipelago. This southerly route was known to have

Adopting the Local Ways

Part of Amundsen's success came from adopting local customs that allowed the native Inuit populations to thrive in the Arctic. In Greenland, Amundsen had purchased twenty sled dogs, which he used for overland transportation during the expedition. This technique, adopted from the Inuit, was much easier than having men pull heavy sleds.

In his first encounter with the Netsilik Inuit, both parties were armed. Amundsen instructed his men to throw down their guns, and the Inuit group threw down their bows and arrows in response. "It is remarkable how accurately two men can communicate who do not speak a word of a common language," Amundsen wrote of the meeting.

The Inuit settled near the crew at Gjøahavn. The Norwegians traded with the Netsilik Inuit for clothing and footwear in exchange for metal goods they had brought to trade, including needles, knives, and empty tin cans. Some items they brought back to Europe for museum collections.

Amundsen described Inuit clothing in his journal:

> Wool underwear gathers all perspiration and will soon make the outside clothing wet. Dressed entirely in reindeer skin, like the Eskimo, and with the clothing loose enough on the body to let the air circulate between the layers, one will as a rule keep the clothing dry… Skins are absolutely wind-proof, which is of course a very important point."

The Inuit also taught them how to build snow houses and hunt on the ice.

When Amundsen and his crew left, they gave the Inuit the wood from their winter house and observatories, a wonderful gift in a tree-less region.

Chapter 3

Goods and Services

When European explorers and rulers first sought a northwest passage, they envisioned a shortcut to Asia through which they could transport spices, gold, and all sorts of treasure. That passage was found, but the dream trade failed to follow.

According to the Department of Environment and Natural Resources of Canada's Northwest Territories, only four vessels per year made it through the Northwest Passage in the 1980s. Today, that number is about thirty per year. Most are icebreakers or adventurers, not commercial shipping vessels.

In this chapter, we'll discuss what governments and merchants hoped to trade, followed by the few commercial trading voyages that have passed through in recent years.

Opposite: *Nuclear icebreakers can break through ice as deep as 13 feet (3.9 m). Only Russia has nuclear icebreakers at present.*

The Imagined Trade

Very little has been traded thus far through the Northwest Passage. The Northwest Passage is simply too hazardous at present time to be used as a mainstream shipping route. The southern routes of the passage are too shallow for large commercial ships to navigate. The northern sea routes are deeper, but dangerous ice conditions present hazards even in the (short) summers. Wind and ocean currents cause the ice to shift. These ice shifts make a channel clear one week and blocked the next. Ice conditions change day to day, even hour to hour.

When explorers first sought the passage, however, they imagined transporting cargo ships filled with great riches through the northwestern sea route. The primary good they sought was spices. They also hoped to trade tea, **porcelain**, textiles, and other luxury goods and natural products found in the East Indies, China, Japan, and India.

Spices

Spices were among the most desired goods from the East Indies. Before sea routes were discovered, trade routes extended from the Far East through India and Arabia, into the Near East and the Mediterranean, and finally into Europe. Spices were passed off from leg to leg. Each merchant added their fee, and the price of spices was exorbitant by the time they reached Europe. Sailing directly to the Far East cut out the middlemen and significantly reduced the cost of goods.

In the 1500s, ships such as those commanded by Ferdinand Magellan and Sir Francis Drake brought back cargoes of cloves, cinnamon, mace, nutmeg, and black pepper. These spices were used for culinary and medicinal purposes. "A passion for spices took possession of Europe, and is one of the most singular of the manias with which mankind seem to be periodically affected," states an article in the well-respected London *Quarterly Review* in 1862. "The true elixir of life was believed to have been at length discovered."

In the sixteenth century, the Spanish and Portuguese controlled the East Indies spice trade. In 1595, the Dutch sent a voyage led by Cornelis de Houtman to the East Indies to find direct access to the spices they so greatly desired. The first voyage brought back enough black pepper to cover its costs. A second voyage brought back an even greater cargo of spices. The Dutch had conflicts and skirmishes with the Spanish and Portuguese along the way. However, they were able to stake a powerful claim in the East Indies spice trade.

The high demand for spices and the lucrative nature of the trade led to the formation of **joint-stock companies**, a type of business entity in which investors own shares of the company. (Joint-stock companies were created to fund endeavors that required huge amounts of capital. They are the predecessors of modern corporations.)

The Dutch East India Company was founded in 1602 with headquarters on Java in modern Indonesia. It was the world's first multinational corporation, and it lasted for two centuries.

Each year, it sent two to three fleets to bring back spices from the East Indies. On the return voyage, they brought goods such as silk and cotton from India and porcelain, silk, and tea from China. The company thrived and made the Netherlands very wealthy. This wealth translated into funding for scientific and artistic endeavors. At this time, the Netherlands boasted the famous artists Rembrandt and Vermeer and the world's first microbiologist, Antonie van Leeuwenhoek.

Similarly, the British East India Company was incorporated by royal charter in 1600 and officially structured as a joint-stock company in 1612. The company was made up of London merchants who sought to profit on the spice trade.

Because the Dutch controlled the East Indies, the British East India Company focused primarily on India. There, it traded in cotton and silk, indigo, and spices.

Until British Parliament passed the Regulating Act of 1773, the East India Company ruled the British Empire's colonies in the Far East. The East India Company operated until 1873.

The French also started a French East India Company in 1664 that oversaw French trade with India, the Far East, and eastern Africa. Unlike the merchant-founded companies of the Dutch and British, the French East India Company was established by a finance minister to King Louis XIV. The king was its largest investor.

Tea

Another popular import from the Far East was tea. Portuguese merchants first brought tea home from the Far East. It was expensive and exotic, which made it a popular beverage with the royalty in Portugal. By the middle of the seventeenth century, tea was a popular beverage in Portugal. By then, tea had also become popular in the Netherlands.

In 1662, Catherine of Braganza, a Portuguese royal, married King Charles II of England. Catherine enjoyed drinking tea. It quickly became a popular drink at court before spreading among the English upper classes and eventually all of society.

Catherine's dowry included the port city of Bombay, which is today known as Mumbai. King Charles II rented Bombay to the British East India Company for just £10 a year. The city became the British East India Company's Indian headquarters until 1708. It was an important part of the company's tea trade.

Tea was promoted as a medical good both by physicians and by marketing campaigns from companies such as the Dutch East India Company. Of course, it was in these companies' best interest to do so because they profited from the tea trade.

By the 1720s, tea had gained favor over coffee in England. Coffee was imported from places like Yemen and the Near East, where Europeans had less knowledge and control over the supply. Coffee was thus a more unpredictable good with higher prices while tea prices remained stable and within British control. According to historian Woodruff Smith, these factors may have been the reason English companies like Twinings chose to focus on tea rather than coffee.

Tea became the hot beverage of choice at home. Taking teatime became a hallmark of respectability and a daily ritual for England's genteel classes. Drinking tea even became a patriotic act by the end of the eighteenth century as consumption supported the British Empire's interests and commerce abroad.

Porcelain

In addition to spices and tea, another major import from Asia was porcelain. Porcelain is a strong, translucent ceramic that is both finer and stronger

Porcelain was often carried at the bottom of ships because it could get wet without being destroyed.

than regular pottery. Chinese porcelain was first introduced to Europe in the fourteenth century. After the Portuguese established the first trade routes to the Far East, Chinese potters began to produce porcelain objects specifically for the Western market.

When porcelain was first introduced, it was scarce and considered a luxury item. Some porcelain objects were even mounted in silver, showing their esteemed position in wealthy households. Once porcelain became more common, however, Europeans began to seek porcelain versions of daily goods, such as mugs and candlesticks. Models of these everyday European household items were sent to China to be copied and produced in porcelain.

Silk, Incense, and More

Spices, tea, and porcelain were major commodities in the European trade in the East Indies. So, too, was a European demand for Chinese silks. Metal work, incense, and ivory were other popular trade goods. In the seventeenth and eighteenth centuries, the interest in Asian goods inspired a new style called **chinoiserie**. This style was the imitation of Chinese patterns and techniques in Western art, wallpaper, furniture, and architecture.

The East Indies, China, India, and Japan had objects that delighted the European senses. The English and the Dutch both had massive trade operations in the region, but the Dutch had primary control of the East Indies and their spices. This Dutch monopoly drove other European nations, primarily the English, to search for a new route to the East Indies where they hoped to find yet untapped islands and riches.

The Actual Trade

Very little international trade has actually taken place through the Northwest Passage due to its dangers. However, there have been a few successful voyages.

From the first transit in 1906 until 1969, there was only one ship every ten years that managed to complete the Northwest Passage route. The first commercial ship to make the trip was the SS *Manhattan*, an oil tanker that made a test run across the Northwest Passage. Accompanied by four icebreakers, it navigated from east to west and back again in 1969. It carried one symbolic barrel of oil but was otherwise empty.

In the following decades, transits increased due to the availability of icebreakers and strong ships able to withstand the Arctic conditions. There were four complete transits per year in the 1980s. This number grew to between twenty and thirty complete transits

CHARLETON, M.D.

Chapter 4

The Major Players

Over four centuries of exploration, many explorers, sponsors, organizations, and institutions played a role in discovering the Northwest Passage. In fact, so many people were instrumental to the discovery that it is not possible in the scope of this book to go into detail about each. Instead, we will highlight some of the most significant people and organizations.

Important Explorers

Some of the most significant explorers in the search for a northwest passage include Sir Martin Frobisher, Sir William Parry, and Roald Amundsen. Frobisher was the first English explorer to look for such a passage. Parry made it farther west above the Arctic Circle than any explorer before him and set leadership standards for Arctic expeditions. Finally,

Opposite: *Frobisher's focus on bringing back gold severely limited the exploratory nature of his second and third voyages.*

Roald Amundsen was the first to make it through the Northwest Passage.

Sir Martin Frobisher

Martin Frobisher was born in 1535 in Yorkshire, England, to a well-connected family. Frobisher himself was hardly literate, and due to a violent and undisciplined nature, he was sent off to sea as a teenager.

His taste for violence showed through in the 1560s, during which Frobisher worked as a **privateer** with a license from the queen. As a privateer, Frobisher captured French merchant ships in the English Channel. He toed the line between privateering and piracy, and Frobisher was arrested and imprisoned several times.

Frobisher was a bold commander and skilled navigator, however, which were favorable traits in an Arctic explorer. In 1576, Queen Elizabeth of England approved a voyage to find a northwest passage, and Frobisher was appointed commander. He sailed with three ships, though due to the dangers of the Davis Strait only one made it through.

When Frobisher returned from his first voyage, he brought back claims of gold on Baffin Island as well as an Inuit captive. The misfortunate Inuk died soon after reaching England due to lack of disease resistance, while Frobisher became a national hero for having discovered gold. In Frobisher's second voyage, he brought back three Inuit captives. The Inuit, taken from their families and home, died within a month.

When it was revealed that the ore brought back from Baffin Island was not gold after all, Frobisher's explorations into the Northwest Passage were over. He struggled to find work for several years afterward, but he avoided permanent damage to his reputation by blaming the failure on others.

In 1585, Frobisher served as vice admiral on Sir Francis Drake's West Indies raid. The fleet sailed to the Caribbean, where they plundered Santiago, Santo Domingo, and Cartagena before sailing north to Florida and capturing and destroying St. Augustine. In 1588, Frobisher fought against the Spanish Armada. He continued to work as a commander in the English navy until his death in 1594. Frobisher died at age fifty-five while leading an attack on a Spanish fortress in Brittany, France.

Sir William Parry

Rear Admiral Sir William Parry was born in December of 1790 in Bath, England. His father was a doctor, and Parry was meant to study medicine as well. However, in 1803, Parry had the opportunity to sail on the *Ville de Paris* along with a family friend, Admiral Sir William Cornwallis. England was in the beginning of the Napoleonic Wars with France. Therefore, the navy was eager for recruits of any age. With Parry on board, the *Ville de Paris* patrolled the English Channel to defend against an invasion by Napoleon.

Parry continued on in the navy and was promoted to lieutenant in 1810. In 1813, he published a book called *Nautical Astronomy by Night*. The book was successful and became widely read in the navy.

When the Napoleonic Wars ended in 1815, many men who had served England during wartime were now available to search for the lucrative Northwest Passage. Parry's first expedition was with Captain John Ross. That mission ended sooner than Parry

Sir William Parry was the first explorer to deliberately winter in the Arctic.

would have liked when Ross declared that a chain of mountains blocked passage through Lancaster Sound. Parry, behind Ross in a slower ship, did not see these mountains and was (rightfully) unconvinced that the Lancaster Sound was landlocked.

In 1819, Parry returned to Lancaster Sound in command of two ships, the *Hecla* and the *Griper*.

A New Winter Standard

Parry's crew spent the winter of 1819–1820 on Melville Island. They had no idea they would set a new standard for Arctic expeditions. Parry's schedule for the men became the model for all Arctic expeditions going forward.

The crew built an observatory on shore and kept regular scientific observations. Each day the men walked along the shore or ran laps on the deck, "keeping step to a tune on the organ, or, not unfrequently, to a song of their own singing," Parry wrote in his journal.

They had twice daily inspections of their cleanliness and warmth of their clothing. In the evenings, the men danced, sang, and played games. The officers read, wrote, played chess, and played the flute or violin. Every half hour through the night, the ships' quartermasters inspected below decks to ensure that the fires and lights burned safely.

Every two weeks, the officers performed in a costumed theater production that gave the crew "infinite amusement," Parry wrote. "Perhaps for the first time since theatrical entertainments were invented, more than one or two plays were performed, on board the *Hecla*, with the thermometer below zero on the stage." The crews also enjoyed "great amusement" from the expedition's weekly newspaper, called the *North Georgia Gazette and Winter Chronicle*.

"Especial care was taken, during the time the sun was below the horizon, to preserve the strictest regularity in the time of our meals, and in the various occupations which engaged our attention during the day … [this] prevented this kind of life, so novel to us in reality, from appearing very inconvenient," Parry wrote. His schedule kept the men healthy, fit, busy, and amused. In doing so, he avoided both disease and dissension.

After wintering in the Arctic, they made it as far as 113°46'W the following year. His crew won a £5,000 reward from the British government for this feat. They returned home in the fall of 1820 when they realized they had made it only 60 miles (96.5 km) in seven weeks, and they would unlikely be able to maintain their remarkable health and wellness through another winter in the Arctic.

Parry went on two more voyages in search of a northwest passage in 1821–1823 and 1824–1825. However, he never made it as far west as he had in the unusually light ice of 1819. In 1827 Parry attempted to reach the North Pole over ice and though he failed, his record of reaching 82°45'N was not surpassed for almost fifty years.

In 1826, Parry married Isabella Stanley, the daughter of a baron. In 1829, Parry was knighted for his services in pursuit of a northwest passage. He took a four-year assignment in Australia working for the Australian Agricultural Company. Eventually, he became the lieutenant-governor of Greenwich Hospital, a permanent home for retired navy sailors. After his first wife died, he married Catharine Hankinson. Parry died in 1855.

Roald Amundsen

Roald Amundsen was known for many different polar expeditions and navigational accomplishments. Amundsen was born in Borge, Norway, in 1872. As a youth, Amundsen was eager to become a polar explorer and conditioned himself by cross-country skiing, bathing in Norwegian fjords, and sleeping with the windows open in winter. When he attended university, he initially studied medicine to please his

Amundsen was called "the last of the Vikings" and is considered one of the greatest polar explorers in human history.

mother. When she died, he switched his focus to the sea. On his first expedition in 1897, he sailed with a Belgian expedition that became the first to winter in Antarctica. When he returned, he began preparations for his navigation of the Northwest Passage.

After sailing through the Northwest Passage, Amundsen sailed to Antarctica and using sled dogs, became the first to reach the South Pole on December 14, 1911. After the success of his Antarctica trip, Amundsen started a shipping business.

He later flew over the North Pole in a dirigible in 1926. (A dirigible is a type of powered, lighter-than-air airship.) In 1928, Amundsen died attempting to rescue Umberto Nobile, one of his companions from that 1926 flight, who had crashed in a dirigible accident near Spitsbergen.

Influential Institutions

Throughout the search for a northwest passage, various organizations funded and directed the expeditions.

Mercantile Groups

Initially, expeditions to look for a northwest passage were funded largely by mercantile groups and private investors. These financers hoped to be repaid through the gold, spices, tea, and other riches from Asia that they imagined would be brought through the discovered trade route.

Frobisher's first expedition was financed largely by Michael Lok. Lok was the director of the Muscovy Company, an English trading company. Frobisher's second voyage was financed by the Company of Cathay, which had been granted a charter as well as some funding from Queen Elizabeth I.

Another group of merchants and British nobility financed many of the early Northwest Passage discovery expeditions. The group requested a charter from King James I of England under the name "the

Company of the Merchant Discoverers of the North-West Passage." The charter request asked to be treated as "a corporate body and to be invested with powers and capacities ... so that the trade through that passage may be managed with some order and government." The group had previously paid for Henry Hudson's voyage in 1610. As an official chartered organization, they aimed to finance expeditions that would complete the exploratory work Hudson's expeditions began.

The Company of the Merchant Discoverers of the North-West Passage went on to fund the expeditions of Thomas Button in 1612, Robert Bylot and William Baffin in 1615, and Baffin again in 1616.

Hudson's Bay Company

In 1659, the French explorers Pierre-Esprit Radisson and Medard Chouart, Sieur des Groseilliers became the first Europeans to explore the Hudson Bay region. They found that the area was rich with beaver furs.

The governor of New France prohibited Radisson and Groseilliers from trading in the Hudson Bay region. Instead, the two Frenchmen brought their vision of a European fur trade in the Hudson Bay to the English royalty. In 1669, King Charles II's cousin Prince Rupert organized a voyage to the Hudson Bay and returned with a ship filled with furs.

After the success of the first voyage, Prince Rupert and a group of wealthy investors founded the **Hudson's Bay Company** (HBC) in May of 1670. (The original name of the company was the "Company of Adventurers Trading into Hudson Bay.") At the time, the king gave almost a million and a half square miles (3,884,982 sq km) surrounding the Hudson Bay to

The king's charter of 1670 gave the HBC land equal to more than 40 percent of the modern nation of Canada.

the HBC. The king believed he had the right to grant the land as he was the first Christian monarch to claim the region. However, the land was already inhabited by Canada's **First Nations**.

The company operated fur trade posts from Newfoundland in eastern Canada to Vancouver Island in western Canada and as far north as the Arctic. Typically, these forts were located where rivers flowed into the Hudson Bay. This made them easily accessible for inland fur traders and sea-faring buyers.

The HBC wasn't particularly eager to help explorers looking for a northwest trade route. They feared its discovery would negatively impact their business. Additionally, all of their resources went toward establishing trade and building forts and outposts.

For a time, their resources also went toward battling for control of the forts with the French.

The English temporarily lost control of the Hudson Bay outposts during the Queen Anne's War with France (1702–1713). They regained the posts after the Treaty of Utrecht in 1713. The HBC sent James Knight, a senior trader with a thirst for finding the Northwest Passage, to reestablish trade.

In 1718 Knight convinced the HBC to finance a sea voyage in search of a northwest passage. He contributed one-eighth of the funding himself. The voyage was approved but with the instructions that Knight avoid stopping at any HBC posts and stay above 64 degrees N. Knight set sail, but after reaching Marble Island, he and his crew were never heard from again.

In 1741, an HBC captain named Christopher Middleton took a commission as captain on a navy expedition looking for a northwest passage. Again the HBC gave orders to prevent Middleton from sailing in the southern parts of the Hudson Bay or wintering at its posts. Middleton knew that he could not afford the same fate as Knight suffered. He was able to negotiate such that the HBC reversed its order and allowed Middleton's ship to winter at its posts.

In the Discovery of North-West Passage Act of 1744 (passed in 1745), the British Parliament decreed that all British subjects were required to provide help and assistance to the explorers when needed. In the following decades, the HBC made thorough searches of the Hudson Bay coastline for any possible passage.

They also sent men north over land and rivers to look for evidence there of a northwest passage.

Most significantly, the company financed the voyages of Samuel Hearne, who traveled north using dogs and sledges as well as snowshoes to map the North American northern coastline.

The British Admiralty

In the early nineteenth century the **Admiralty**, the group in command of the British Royal Navy, became a significant financer and organizer of Northwest Passage discovery missions.

Initially, the Admiralty did not see a role for the navy in discovery missions. That view changed over time. This is evidenced by its decision in the 1770s to send Captain James Cook into the Pacific to search for a southern continent and north in pursuit of a passage over North America into the Atlantic.

In 1817, the Admiralty approved the expeditions of Commander John Ross and Lieutenant William Parry through Baffin Bay. In 1818, Ross and Parry sailed on strengthened whaling ships laden with tin canned food. They also carried a variety of scientific and astronomical instruments for scientific observations. The ships were well outfitted overall, and separations were kept between officers and crew.

The Admiralty sent many voyages in search of a northwest passage over the next several decades, including additional voyages led by Parry and John Franklin. Before Franklin's tragic sea voyage, the Admiralty sent him on two equipment-laden, unfortunate Arctic expeditions over land in 1819–1822 and 1825–1827.

The Admiralty financed the final voyage of John Franklin in 1845. During this expedition, all men died.

Over the next decade, the Admiralty sent many more ships on Franklin search and rescue—and then simply search—missions.

Important Inventors

One of the major inventions that affected the search for the Northwest Passage was the invention of tin canned foods.

The Tin Can

Throughout the search for the Northwest Passage, crews suffered from debilitating and sometimes fatal cases of scurvy. The powerful British, French, and Dutch navies also struggled with scurvy, as did armies. Whether for missions by sea or by land, by the late eighteenth century, there was a pressing need for a way to store and preserve a more diverse array of foods for long trips.

Tin canned food was invented in England, but by the 1920s, the United States was the biggest producer of canned goods.

In 1795, the French military offered a ₣12,000 prize to an inventor who created a method for preserving food. (That's equivalent to about $33,000 today; the franc [₣] was the French currency prior to switching to the euro.) That same year, the French chef Nicolas Francois Appert began experimenting with a solution. Fourteen years later, Appert won the prize for his method of boiling food such as partridges, peas, raspberries, and broth in champagne bottles.

Soon after, a French man named Phillippe de Girard invented a method to preserve food in tin cans that would be less likely to break. Girard approached British merchant Peter Durand to patent his idea in England. Yet Durand patented it in his own name instead. Durand then sold the patent to the British scientist Bryan Donkin and kept the money.

Donkin had previously patented the first steel pen as an alternative to the quill and a device that measured the speed of machines. He had also created a papermaking machine and opened eighteen papermaking mills in England. These endeavors helped fund his new canning business. Donkin built a factory near the Thames River in Bermondsey (in south London) and spent two years refining Girard's tin canning method. He was joined in his venture by John Hall and John Gamble.

Donkin and Gamble presented their canned beef to the duke of Kent at Kensington Palace in 1813. The duke, the queen of England, the prince regent, and other British nobility tasted the new product. They gave it high praise, and that same year the Admiralty bought 156 pounds (70 kg) of canned food. Soon, other companies began selling tin canned food as well.

At first, the canned food industry suffered significant quality control issues. In one quality control inspection, inspectors found rotten meat, canned dog parts, and organs from diseased animals in a shipment of cans destined for the navy.

The ill-fated expedition led by John Franklin in 1847, for example, carried food from a problematic supplier, Stephen Goldner. Goldner's canned food was of such poor quality and sanitation that he was eventually banned from selling to the navy.

Over time, the quality problems decreased as the market and regulators demanded higher quality goods. Their availability allowed Northwest Passage explorers to carry enough food for years, including the vegetables needed to prevent scurvy.

Chapter 5

The Effects of the Northwest Passage

The Northwest Passage is not yet a bustling commercial shipping route. Yet the discovery of the passage has had a significant impact on Arctic and near-Arctic **states** (countries).

The Northwest Passage will become increasingly open in the next century. Countries including the United States, Canada, and China are preparing for the political, economic, environmental, and human concerns that come with a new trade route.

In this chapter, we'll focus on the actions nations are taking today in anticipation of the passage's future. In the final chapter, we'll discuss what experts anticipate that future will look like.

Opposite: *Canada's claim over the Northwest Passage is complex and disputed.*

Who Owns the Northwest Passage?

One of the major current issues regarding the Northwest Passage is that of **sovereignty** and whether the waterways around the Canadian Arctic Archipelago are Canada's **internal waters** or international waters. Canada and the United States have opposing opinions on this question. Both countries have significant economic and environmental interests in the region's future.

Canadian Sovereignty

Canada claims **jurisdiction** (the right to make legal decisions and administer justice) over the Arctic waterways based on two major arguments. The first argument is based on its historic ownership of the land around the passage. The second argument is based on how Canada draws its territorial boundary lines. Canada draws its **baseline** (boundary line) around the archipelago. Based on this boundary, the Canadian government says the Northwest Passage should be considered Canada's internal waters. A state has as much jurisdiction over its internal waters as it exercises over its mainland territory. Therefore, it can make laws regarding the use of those internal waters.

Not everyone agrees with Canada's claims. To understand the first claim, we must consider precedents set in settling other international territory disputes. (In legal disputes, precedents are previous legal decisions that can shape future disputes of a similar nature.) According to Artur Kozlowski in the *Polish Yearbook of International Law*:

> The [International Law Commission] postulates that, in examining a claim for historic title, three factors must be examined: (1) the exercise of authority over the area by the State claiming the historic right; (2) the continuity of this exercise of authority; (3) the attitude of foreign States.

In other words, for a state to claim a historic title to a territory, it must prove three things. It must prove it has had jurisdiction of that region. It must have also exercised that jurisdiction for a very long, continuous period of time. Furthermore, other states must recognize that jurisdiction without conflict. States must show evidence of their authority such as legislative, executive, or judicial acts in the region that were conducted publicly and effectively.

A state can also prove a historic claim to a territory if the territory had been surrendered to it by another sovereign state. This is an important part of Canada's historic title claim.

Most of the Arctic Archipelago north of the Canadian mainland was discovered by English and French explorers. In 1763, the Treaty of Paris gave France's land in North America to Great Britain.

In 1867, the British colonies of Canada, Nova Scotia, and New Brunswick were united as the **Dominion** of Canada, a self-governing federal state with four provinces. As a dominion, Canada was largely independent but the British crown handled international diplomacy. In 1870, the Dominion of Canada acquired the lands of the Hudson's Bay Company. It created the province of Manitoba and the Northwest Territories with this acquisition. (The HBC land accounts for more than 40 percent of the modern nation!)

In 1880, all of the remaining British lands in North America were transferred to the Dominion of Canada. This included all islands adjacent to any territories but excluded the British colony of Newfoundland. Canada shed its dominion status in 1931, and Newfoundland became part of Canada in 1949 as the province of Newfoundland and Labrador. Today, Canada has ten provinces and three territories.

Through this historic acquisition of its territory, Canada's government believes that the archipelago islands discovered by the European expeditions and the surrounding Arctic waters are now part of Canada.

Canada's historic title rationale is the weaker of its two arguments. Other states, including the United States, have protested Canada's claims to sovereignty over the Arctic waters.

According to one of Canada's leading experts on the Arctic, Donat Pharand, nobody specifically took possession of the Arctic waters when British and Canadian explorers claimed land in the Arctic Archipelago. Additionally, Canada has been unable to force foreign ships to obtain authorization before passing through the Northwest Passage. This suggests that it does not have full control over the region.

Canada's most powerful argument, that the Arctic waters are internal waters, is based on the 1982 United Nations Convention on the Law of the Sea (UNCLOS).

According to the UNCLOS, a coastal state's internal waters include all of the water within its baseline (an official political boundary). This baseline must be

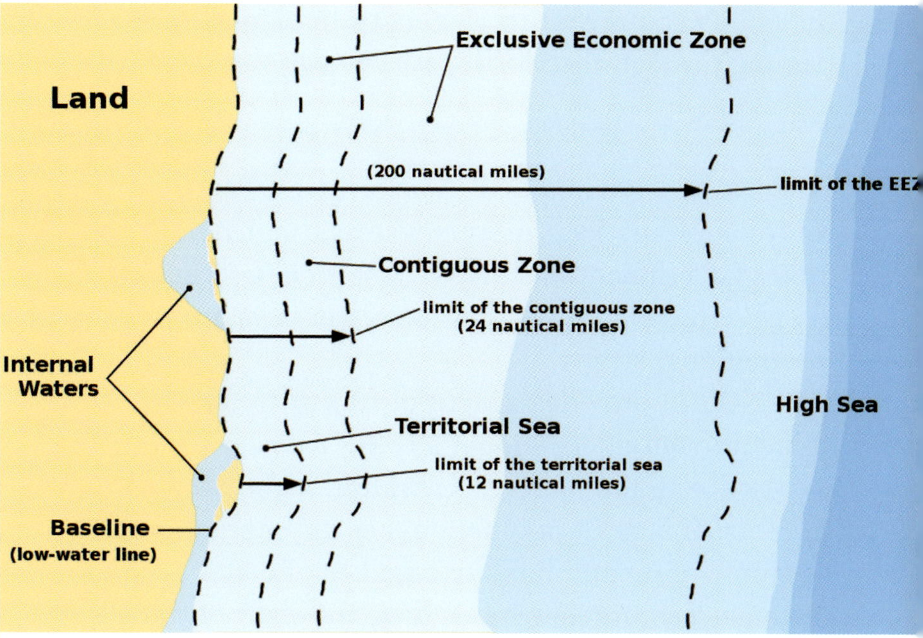

Baselines must closely follow a state's coastline, except when veering to enclose a fringe of islands along the coast.

drawn at the low-water mark of a state's coastline. If there are islands along the coast, the state can extend its baseline to include the water around those islands. (See the accompanying diagram for an example of a baseline.)

States can claim complete sovereignty over their internal waters. A state can pass laws and regulate the use of the water (be it ocean, bay, lake, or river) just as it does on its land possessions. Foreign ships have no right to pass through a state's internal waters.

The Canadian government drew its baseline around the Arctic Archipelago. Thus, the Canadian government holds that all waterways on the landward side of that baseline, including the Northwest Passage routes, are Canadian internal waters. The government claims the ability to enforce its laws over those waterways and the ability to prevent foreigners or foreign ships from passing through the Northwest Passage.

International Waters

While Canada claims that the Northwest Passage routes are Canadian internal waters, the United States government has disputed this claim. The US government argues that the waterways are international straits.

UNCLOS provides a right of transit to foreign ships through international straits. You can see this in practice in the Strait of Gibraltar or the Strait of Hormuz. If a strait is functional as an international maritime route and links two bodies of water such as the high seas, foreign states have the right of transit through the strait. Under this right of transit, foreign ships do not have to request permission to navigate through it.

The Strait of Gibraltar is a 36-mile-long (57.9 km) channel between Spain and Africa that connects the Mediterranean and the Atlantic.

The Antarctic Treaty

The governance of land and waterways in the Antarctic region contrasts the current dispute over the Arctic Archipelago. Looking at how land and waterways are governed in the Antarctic can help explain how countries come to agree about disputed territories.

On December 1, 1959, the twelve countries with active scientific presences in and around Antarctica signed a treating governing the use of Antarctica. (Today, fifty-three nations have signed the treaty.) Some of these countries, including the United States, France, and the United Kingdom, had made previous territorial claims to the Antarctic region. The treaty effectively ended those claims.

The Antarctic Treaty states that the region will only be used for peaceful purposes and that countries will cooperate in scientific endeavors and share observations and results. It does not contain provisions for protecting the Antarctic environment. However, it laid the groundwork for later agreements that are collectively known as the Antarctic Treaty System. The Antarctic Treaty System does include provisions for the conservation of plants, animals, and natural resources. The 1991 Madrid Protocol on Environmental Protection to the Antarctic Treaty, for example, bans mining activities in Antarctica.

Similar measures have been proposed for the Arctic.

As of yet, the Northwest Passage is not entirely functional as an international maritime route. For some, this means that the passage is not an international strait. In turn, this means there is no right of transit. Given that the passage may become a viable maritime route as climate change melts the Arctic sea ice, it's likely that the Northwest Passage will see more international traffic in the future. It could become a functioning international strait in time.

The evolution of the Northwest Passage into an international strait is not inevitable, however. According to Robert Dufresne, an analyst in the Canadian Parliament's Law and Government Division:

> Internationalization is only a possibility, and it is by no means unavoidable. The pull towards internationalization of the Passage could be resisted and countered by Canada, through concrete acts of assertion of sovereignty.

Dufresne refers to Pharand's suggestions for what these acts of assertion of sovereignty could be, writing:

> Measures include ... acquiring a polar icebreaker; developing sea-and-land-based services in the region; completing the setting in place of a radar satellite to monitor surface vessels; ensuring a submarine detection and control capacity; patrolling the regions, ensuring rescue capacity; and creating a deep-water seaport.

In other words, if Canada performs the activities of daily jurisdiction, it will give evidence to support its claim that the Arctic waterways are under its jurisdiction. The activities of daily jurisdiction include providing icebreakers to aid foreign ships crossing the Northwest Passage, providing emergency services to ships in distress, and actively monitoring traffic in the Arctic Archipelago.

The Current State of the Northwest Passage

The United States and Canada are allies and neighbors with a good relationship. Thus, the dispute over the Northwest Passage is one of the biggest issues between them. There is no resolution as of yet.

In 1988, however, the United States and Canada signed an "Agreement Between Canada and the United States on Arctic Cooperation." The agreement states that the United States and Canada recognize their shared interests and responsibilities as neighboring Arctic states. It also recognizes the benefits of cooperation. To this end, the United States and Canada agree to cooperate on Arctic development and security. They also agree to share research information regarding the marine environment.

The agreement further states that the United States will get Canada's consent for all American icebreaker navigation through waters that Canada claims as internal. Notably, the treaty also says that the signature and execution of the agreement does not affect "the respective positions of the Governments of the United States and of Canada on the Law of the Sea in this or other maritime areas."

In other words, the United States agreed to ask before sending an icebreaker through the Northwest Passage. Yet it took care to state that doing so doesn't change its opinion that the Northwest Passage waterways are an international strait. Meanwhile, Canada recognizes this and continues to assert that the Arctic waterways are internal waters.

It's important to note that the agreement covers only icebreakers. This means that it doesn't address passage by commercial vessels.

The United States, the European Union, and Canada are not the only entities politically or economically invested in the future of the Northwest Passage. The Chinese government is making preparations for future shipping through the Northwest Passage.

The Chinese government's Maritime Safety Administration announced in April 2016 that it had published a Chinese-language *Arctic Navigation Guide (Northwest Passage)*. The guide affirms China's intent to ship cargo through the Northwest Passage as the polar ice caps continue to melt. But it also shows the complexity involved in doing so. The guide includes information on navigating through sea ice and Arctic weather.

According to Yin Jingbao, a maritime economics researcher quoted in *The Globe and Mail*, the main cargo will be containers hauled from China to North America's Eastern Seaboard. However, he also noted it will take quite some time before Chinese commercial shipping begins.

If China does begin to send ships through the passage, it could present a new challenge to Canada's claim that the Arctic waterways are internal waters and not a functioning international strait. As of yet,

China has not taken an explicit stance on Canada's sovereignty over the Northwest Passage.

Impact of the Sovereignty Dispute

There have been no outright conflicts over Canada's sovereignty claim over the Northwest Passage. However, there have been very tangible effects from the dispute.

In the 1950s, several Inuit families (around ninety people total) were forcibly relocated from their homes. They were moved from Inukjuak in northern Quebec to Canada's **High Arctic**. (The High Arctic is a region of the Arctic that has a shorter growing season, colder summers, and much less plant and animal life than the Low Arctic region.) The families were divided into two settlements, Grise Fiord and Resolute. These became Canada's northernmost communities.

The government's official explanation was that the relocation was designed to bring the Inuit to a place of abundant game and fish. However, there is not abundant game and fish in those regions. Many people suspect that the relocation was to assert Canada's sovereignty in the Arctic and jurisdiction over the waterways of the Northwest Passage.

The families were left without proper shelter or supplies in a cold tundra with limited wildlife, completely dark winters, and no access to health care. The government promised the Inuit could come home after two years if they weren't happy but did not fulfill this promise.

In 2010, the Canadian government acknowledged and apologized for its lack of planning and failure to keep its promises. Yet it maintains that the move was done in the best interest of the relocated Inuit.

In the official apology, Canada's minister of Indian and Northern Affairs John Duncan said:

> The families were separated from their home communities and extended families by more than a thousand kilometers. They were not provided with adequate shelter and supplies. They were not properly informed of how far away and how different from Inukjuak their new homes would be, and they were not aware that they would be separated into two communities once they arrived in the High Arctic. Moreover, the Government failed to act on its promise to return anyone that did not wish to stay in the High Arctic to their old homes.

Canada's government created a $10 million fund called the Arctic Exile Relocatee Trust that gave annual payouts to the survivors of the relocation and their direct descendants. The *Toronto Star* reports that the payments were as high as $10,000 or $15,000 per individual in the initial years. Now, the payments have dropped significantly to just a few hundred dollars per year.

While the relocated Inuit suffered in their first years there, the communities learned the beluga whale migration routes and hunted across thousands of miles to survive.

Today, Grise Fiord, the more northerly of the two locations at 76°25'N, has a population of 141 people, 95 percent of whom are Inuit. Grise Fiord is the Norwegian name given to the region by the Norwegian explorer Otto Sverdrup. The **Inuktitut** name for the region is Aujuittuq, or "place that never thaws."

Grise Fiord is 721 miles (1,160.3 km) north of the Artic Circle and experiences twenty-four-hour sunshine from April 22 to August 20. However, in the cold, dark winters, the temperature can drop to -58°F (-50°C). The sea is frozen for ten months of the year.

Resolute, meanwhile, is called Qausuittuq in Inuktitut, or "place with no dawn" because of its long winter night. It is the second most northerly community in Canada at 74°43'N and is also called Resolute Bay. There are 242 inhabitants, 80 percent of whom are Inuit. Like Grise Fiord, it experiences nearly four months of constant daylight in the summer but plunges into darkness from mid-November to February.

Looking Forward

In many ways, the Northwest Passage is a trade route waiting to happen. The primary impact of its discovery thus far has been to raise questions of sovereignty over the Arctic waters and whether foreign nations need Canada's permission to pass through. Those questions have not yet been settled at this time.

There are many other considerations for the future of the Northwest Passage, however. These include when the passage will become ice-free enough to support regular commercial traffic, the logistics necessary to make the route safer for ships, and the impact of Arctic shipping on the environment.

Chapter 6

The Future of the Northwest Passage

The Northwest Passage has always been a dream of the future. When it was first envisioned, nobody knew for sure whether or not such a passage existed from the Atlantic to the Pacific, but explorers were determined to find it. Over centuries, explorer after explorer hoped that he would be the first to make it through.

Amundsen triumphed in 1906 and yet, more than one hundred years since his voyage, trade is still a dream of the future. This future opportunity comes at the hands of global warming and melting Arctic ice, which also bring negative consequences to the Arctic and the world below.

Given the rate of melting ice, it is likely that the Northwest Passage will become a more viable trade

Opposite: *According to NASA, the amount of Arctic sea ice (by square mile) is declining at a rate of 13.3 percent per decade.*

route in the next century. Canada, the United States, and other countries are preparing for that day.

The Opening of the Northwest Passage

The future of the Northwest Passage is dependent on how climate change affects the ice in the Arctic Archipelago. The **Arctic Council**'s Protection of the Arctic Marine Environment work group has put together a document called the Arctic Marine Shipping Assessment (ASMA). ASMA says the Arctic may have ice-free summers by the middle of this century. However, not all areas of the Arctic will be affected in the same way.

The Impact of Climate Change

For millennia, the Arctic has been an ice-covered ocean surrounded by treeless, frozen land. Today, the Arctic is changing rapidly in response to climate change caused by humans and the carbon dioxide released into the atmosphere by the vast quantities of oil, coal, and natural gas they burn. Climate change impacts the Arctic more quickly and more severely than it does the rest of the world. In fact, the Arctic is warming nearly twice as fast as the global average warming.

Ice and snow in the Arctic reflect the sun's energy back into space. As the ice and snow melt due to warming temperatures, the Arctic contains a decreasing amount of reflective surfaces. Instead, it contains increasingly more absorbent surfaces, primarily exposed rock and water.

During the summer, the rocks and open water absorb and retain heat from the sun. The absorbed

The albedo of a surface is measured on a scale of 0 (perfect absorption of energy) to 1 (perfect reflection of energy).

heat further increases the temperature of the Arctic Ocean. The name for this compounded warming effect is the albedo effect (albedo is the amount of solar energy reflected from Earth back into space).

According to an Arctic Climate Impact Assessment (ACIA), released by the Arctic Council at a meeting in 2004, Arctic sea ice has been declining for the past five decades. The average sea ice thickness has been decreasing. The amount of old ice (ice that has remained frozen for more than one year) is decreasing. Overall, satellite data shows that Arctic sea ice coverage in September has declined by 30 percent over the past thirty years. (September is used for comparisons because it's the month that marks the end of summer and the peak of annual ice melt.)

According to various ACIA models, the Arctic may be ice-free for a period each summer as soon as 2040.

Some of the resulting changes from an ice-free Arctic could have slowing effects. An increase in trees that remove carbon from the air is one example. However, the National Oceanic and Atmospheric Administration (NOAA) predicts that the overall effect of global warming will be that the Arctic never returns to its previous climate conditions.

While climate change will reduce the ice cover and the thickness of the ice, it will not make the Northwest Passage an absolutely safe, predictable route. Sea ice is always variable. There may continue to be summers with heavy ice conditions even among periods of generally low-ice summers. Along with warming ocean temperatures come shifts in **pack ice** (large masses of mobile ice) toward the south and an increase of drifting **multiyear ice** (ice more than two summers old). These effects create new blockages and navigational hazards for ships passing through.

There are several different routes through the Northwest Passage. The fastest route (from Baffin Bay through the McClure Strait and into the Beaufort Sea) is also the most northern route. Even in summers in which the Arctic Ocean is free of ice, climate models show that the northern part of the Arctic Archipelago will still contain multiyear ice. This ice is meters thick, very hard, and dangerous.

The southern route through Peel Sound is more likely to be free of ice on a regular basis (it's already been open in recent summers). However, the southern route is not as direct as the northern route. Also, the passageways are narrower and shallower, which prohibits large vessels from passing through.

Of course, climate change affects much more in the Arctic than the Northwest Passage. Climate change also has a strong impact on Arctic flora and fauna. As snow and ice melt, the habitats of Arctic natives like the polar bear are disappearing.

At the same time, the increased carbon dioxide (CO_2) in the atmosphere is changing the composition of the Arctic Ocean. About 25 to 30 percent of the CO_2 released by burning fossil fuels is absorbed by the ocean.

Prior to industrialization, the amount of carbon dioxide in the atmosphere and the ocean was balanced. The Smithsonian Ocean Portal estimates that since the beginning of the Industrial Revolution, however, the ocean has absorbed about 525 billion tons of CO_2 from the atmosphere, or 22 million tons per day.

The growing amount of CO_2 in the ocean is increasing the acidity of the ocean. Overall, according to the World Wildlife Fund, the world's oceans are 30 percent more acidic than they were before the Industrial Revolution. The Arctic Ocean and other cold oceans are acidifying twice as fast as average.

The increased acidity of the oceans affects the development of shells and skeletons. These include phytoplankton, zooplankton, oysters, mussels, and corals. Increased acidity makes it harder for marine animals to build those structures, and the existing structures dissolve more rapidly in the acidic seawater. This impacts other species higher on the food chain, which depend on coral for shelter and small shellfish for food.

Environmental Impact of Increased Traffic

The increased amount of CO_2 isn't the only challenge the Arctic environment faces. Many natives and scientists fear that increased traffic through the

Male narwhals can grow tusks nearly 9 feet (2.7 m) long that scientists believe may be used to impress females or to fight other males.

Northwest Passage will have significant negative effects on the environment.

With shipping comes the risk of oil and chemical spills. Any spills would introduce highly toxic substances into the oceans. Increased shipping also increases the amount of sound animals are exposed to. Animals like the beluga whale, bowhead whale, and narwhal communicate using sound. The introduction of new sound sources can have negative consequences on their lives.

According to Andrew Hartsig, director of the Ocean Conservancy's Arctic Program, "increased ocean noise can result in habitat displacement, behavioral changes and alterations in the intensity, frequency and intervals of whale calls."

Logistics

Climate models show an icy future for the shorter, northern route of the Northwest Passage. Yet an increase in traffic through the passage is expected to continue. As more ships sail through the Northwest Passage, logistics become increasingly important. The Northwest Passage is in a remote, dangerous, and mercurial part of the globe. It's crucial that there is enough infrastructure and resources to support frequent voyages through the passage.

To understand the infrastructure required to support an Arctic shipping and transit route, it's useful to compare the infrastructure along the Northwest Passage with the infrastructure Russia has in place along the Northeast Passage. The Northeast Passage is considered easier to traverse, and it's supported by better infrastructure.

The most important logistics to have in place are icebreakers and seaports. Icebreakers clear the way for other ships. Seaports provide resources and safe harbor for ships in need.

Icebreakers

Russia has a fleet of at least forty icebreakers ready to clear the way for commercial voyages through the Northern Sea Route over its north coast. The nation also has plans to add eleven more. Six of those are nuclear-powered with 75,000 horsepower in their engines or more, giving the Russians a unique Arctic advantage. In contrast, Canada has fifteen icebreakers to aid vessels through the Arctic. Only two of these are heavy icebreakers.

Icebreakers are not maintained just to clear the way for Arctic commerce. They are also important in defense, rescue missions, and scientific research. It's important that Canada has the ability to support vessels passing through the Northwest Passage, especially in light of its claims to sovereignty over the waterways.

Seaports and Rescue Capacities

Canada currently has no ports along the Northwest Passage that could offer refuge to a ship traveling through. If a ship has a mechanical problem or is overwhelmed from a storm, there is no safe harbor.

In addition to providing assistance to ships, the Coast Guard also supports scientific missions like mapping the Arctic sea floor.

There is also a significant delay in Canada's ability to respond to the crisis.

According to Michael Byers, an international lawyer and expert on Arctic issues, writing for the nationally distributed Canadian newspaper *The Globe and Mail* in 2013:

> Canada's Arctic search-and-rescue capabilities are desperately poor. Our long-range helicopters are based in British Columbia, Nova Scotia and Labrador: each aircraft would take more than a day to fly the 2,500 kilometers to the Northwest Passage, stopping to refuel along the way ... As a point of comparison, Russia has several search-and-rescue stations in the Arctic and is building ten more—each with its own ships and aircraft.

In addition to Russia's rescue capacity, it also has sixteen deep-water seaports along its Arctic coastline that can accommodate large ships.

Canada's lack of deep-water seaports in the Northwest Passage heightens the risks of using the route for commercial purposes. In one recent incident, a Canadian fishing vessel named *Saputi* hit a 16-foot-long (5-meter-long) clump of ice in the Davis Strait. The *Saputi* took on water faster than it could handle. It sent out a distress signal to the Canadian Coast Guard. The Canadian Coast Guard in turn notified the Danish navy in Nuuk, Greenland.

The Danish navy rescued the ship and escorted *Saputi* to Nuuk, a 500-mile (804.6-km) journey. There was no closer Canadian deep-water port.

The Danish navy responding more quickly than the Canadian government to a disaster in Canadian water and bringing the Canadian ship back to Greenland raises questions of how firm Canada's sovereignty over its water actually is. According to Byers, providing seaports as well as icebreakers and other logistics is an important part of Canada's claim. The nation must prove to the United States that it can and will protect the Arctic waters. (And thus show its right to claim sovereignty over those waters.)

A plan is in the works for a seaport in Iqaluit, the capital of the Nunavut territory on Baffin Island. The seaport will be a northern hub for the Canadian military and Coast Guard and is scheduled for completion by 2020.

Human Impact

The commercial use of the Northwest Passage will also affect the Inuit populations who live along it. Some of those potential effects are mentioned above, such as concerns about the environmental impact of increased commercial traffic on the animals they hunt. In turn, Inuits' health and wellness are affected.

However, P. Whitney Lackenbauer, a fellow of the Canadian Defence & Foreign Affairs Institute, writes:

> It is important to note that Inuit, despite their concerns about the human and environmental impacts of shipping, generally look forward to the prospect of increased maritime activity. More shipping will reduce the costs of supplies and improve standards of living in a region

> where limited resupply options have led to $7 litres of milk and $40 packs of diapers.
>
> Alleviating Canada's highest levels of unemployment is equally important, and good paying jobs in the resource sector are predicated on cost-effective access to these resources and an ability to carry them to market. The risks inherent in Arctic shipping must therefore be considered alongside these new opportunities as well.

The future of the Northwest Passage brings many uncertainties, but also many opportunities. For Canada, there is an opportunity to provide icebreakers and seaports to aid foreign vessels. This would demonstrate its active presence and jurisdiction over the Arctic waters. For the Inuit, there is the potential for new jobs and better quality of life. For businesses, there is the potential to get their goods to consumers in less time and for less money.

The future of the Northwest Passage also poses environmental risks and political uncertainties, however. What will Canada or other governing bodies do to regulate the environmental impact of ships passing through the Arctic? Will Canada be able to convince other nations to accept its sovereignty claims over the Arctic waters? These questions, and many more, will be answered in time.

Glossary

Admiralty A former government department responsible for commanding the British Royal Navy.

archipelago A chain or group of islands, such as the chain of islands that make up Japan.

Arctic Circle The region around the North Pole in which the sun does not set on the summer solstice and the sun does not appear on the winter solstice; currently the region above 66°34'N.

Arctic Council An intergovernmental forum consisting of the eight states with land above the Arctic Circle dedicated to promoting cooperation among the Arctic states.

baseline An imaginary line drawn to show a coastal state's coastal boundary (typically drawn at the low water mark).

chinoiserie The imitation of Chinese patterns and techniques, such as bamboo and pagoda motifs, in Western art, furniture, and design.

dominion In the case of the British Commonwealth, a self-governing nation that recognizes the British monarch as the head of state responsible for conducting foreign diplomacy.

First Nations The indigenous inhabitants of Canada that are not Inuit or of mixed indigenous and European settler ancestry.

High Arctic A region of the Arctic that has a shorter growing season, colder summers, and much less plant and animal life than the corresponding Low Arctic region.

Hudson's Bay Company A company founded in 1670 to trade furs around the Hudson Bay in Canada.

ice floe A sheet of floating ice.

internal waters Waters on the landward side of a state's boundary, such as lakes, rivers, and some bays.

Inuit A group of indigenous people in the Arctic spanning Alaska, Canada, and Greenland.

Inuk A single Inuit person.

Inuktitut One of the principal languages spoken by the Inuit throughout the Canadian Arctic.

joint-stock company A business entity in which stock is owned by shareholders; the first known instance of a joint-stock company was formed to fund the search for a trade route to Asia.

jurisdiction The right to make legal decisions and administer justice in a certain region or over certain types of cases.

meridian A line of longitude, such as the 141st Meridian at 141°W.

multiyear ice Ice that has remained frozen through at least two summers, resulting in ice 3 meters (9.8 ft.) thick (or greater).

pack ice Sea ice that is not attached to the shore and thus can drift with the wind, current, or other forces.

pejorative A disparaging term.

pinnace A small boat with sails or oars used to conduct nimble operations for a larger boat, such as trips to shore.

porcelain A very fine, white, translucent ceramic, originally made in China and treasured in Europe.

privateer A person authorized by the government to capture enemy merchant ships (or an armed ship used for this purpose); a licensed pirate.

scurvy A disease caused by a lack of vitamin C that results in fatigue, weakness, bleeding gums, loose teeth, and many other debilitating problems.

soapstone A type of soft rock consisting mostly of talc, used to make carvings, bowls, and other objects.

sovereignty The authority to govern a region.

state In international politics, a state is a political entity governed by a single system of government, such as the country of France or the country of the United States of America.

Further Information

Books

Berton, Pierre. *Exploring the Frozen North*. Markham, ON: Fifth House Publishing, 2006.

Delgado, James. *Across the Top of the World*. Madeira Park, BC: Douglas & McIntyre, 2009.

Gleason, Carrie. *Henry Hudson: Seeking the Northwest Passage*. New York, NY: Crabtree Publishing, 2005.

Websites

Arctic Ecosystem
http://wimedialab.pbslearningmedia.org/resource/ipy07.sci.life.eco.arcticecosys/arctic-ecosystem/
Learn about the Arctic ecosystem from zooplankton to bowhead whales, from ice algae to polar bears, and how everything connects.

Cargo Ships Traverse the World's Oceans
http://www.digitaltrends.com/cool-tech/cargo-ship-interactive-map/
This beautiful interactive map shows shipping activity across the globe over time. See which shipping routes are common, which are rare, and what each ship carries.

Pan Inuit Trails
http://paninuittrails.org/index.html
Explore the network of land, sea, and ice trails the Inuit used to trade a variety of goods and resources.

Tracking Franklin and Amundsen
http://www.pbs.org/wgbh/nova/ancient/tracking-franklin-amundsen.html
Franklin and Amundsen traveled almost the same route to dramatically different ends. Launch the interactive media window to follow along on their journeys.

Videos

"Drone Art: Arctic Wildlife & Landscapes"
https://youtu.be/CIaZaBdYXx4
Take a trip through a section of the Northwest Passage, with footage of beluga whales and polar bears as you go.

"Russian Nuclear Powered Ice Breaker Ship 50 Let Pobedy"
https://www.youtube.com/watch?v=Q6OHHGrVM3g
Follow a Russian icebreaker to the North Pole as it cuts through meters-thick sea ice.

"Sailing the Northwest Passage"
https://www.youtube.com/watch?v=C13AyCekwDw
Follow two explorers as they make the 195th transit of the Northwest Passage. Immerse yourself in the Arctic, view remnants of long-ago explorations, watch icebreakers in action, and more.

Bibliography

Amundsen, Roald. *My Life as An Explorer.* Garden City, NY: Doubleday, Page & Co, 1927.

Arctic Council. "Arctic Marine Shipping Assessment 2009 Report." Retrieved December 12, 2016. http://www.pmel.noaa.gov/arctic-zone/detect/documents/AMSA_2009_Report_2nd_print.pdf.

Bennett, Jennifer, ed. "Ocean Acidification." Smithsonian National Museum of Natural History. Retrieved December 12, 2016. http://ocean.si.edu/ocean-acidification.

Byers, Michael. "Canada's Arctic Nightmare Just Came True." *The Globe and Mail,* September 20, 2013. http://www.theglobeandmail.com/opinion/canadas-arctic-nightmare-just-came-true-the-northwest-passage-is-commercial/article14432440/.

Casselman, Anne. "Will the Opening of the Northwest Passage Transform Global Shipping Anytime Soon?" *Scientific American,* November 10, 2008. https://www.scientificamerican.com/article/opening-of-northwest-passage/.

Dufresne, Robert. "Controversial Canadian Claims over Arctic Waters and Maritime Zones." *Parliamentary Information and Research Service,* January 10, 2008. http://www.lop.parl.gc.ca/content/lop/researchpublications/prb0747-e.pdf.

Duncan, John. "Apology for the Inuit High Arctic Relocation." *Indigenous and Northern Affairs Canada,* September 9, 2015. https://www.aadnc-aandc.gc.ca/eng/1100100016115/1100100016116.

Geoghegan, Tim. "The Story of How the Tin Can Nearly Wasn't." *BBC Magazine,* April 21, 2013. http://www.bbc.com/news/magazine-21689069.

Godoy, Maria. "Tea Tuesdays: How Tea + Sugar Reshaped the British Empire." NPR, April 7, 2015. http://www.npr.org/sections/thesalt/2015/04/07/396664685/tea-tuesdays-how-tea-sugar-reshaped-the-british-empire.

Kozlowski, Artur. "The Legal Construct of Historic Title to Territory in International Law – An Overview." *Polish Yearbook of International Law* no. 30 (2010): 61–100.

Lackenbauer, Whitney, and Adam Lajeunesse. "More Ships in the Northwest Passage Will Boost Our Arctic Claim." *The Globe and Mail,* January 5, 2015. http://www.theglobeandmail.com/opinion/more-ships-in-the-northwest-passage-will-boost-our-arctic-claim/article22294408/.

Macpherson, William, ed. "The Eastern Archipelago." *Quarterly Review* no. 111 (1862): 483–516.

McGarrity, John, and Henning Gloystein. "Northwest Passage Crossed by First Cargo Ship, the Nordic Orion, Heralding New Era of Arctic Commercial Activity." *National Post,* September 27, 2013. http://news.nationalpost.com/news/canada/northwest-passage-crossed-by-first-cargo-ship-the-nordic-orion-heralding-new-era-of-arctic-commercial-activity.

Morrison, David. "The Copper Inuit Soapstone Trade." *Arctic* 44, no. 3 (1991): 239–246.

National Snow & Ice Data Center. "Climate Change in the Arctic." Retrieved December 12, 2016. https://nsidc.org/cryosphere/arctic-meteorology/climate_change.html.

Parry, Sir William Edward. *Journal of a Voyage for the Discovery of a North-west Passage from the Atlantic to the Pacific*. London, UK: J. Murray, 1821.

Rijksmuseum. "1602 Trade with the East: VOC." Retrieved December 13, 2016. https://www.rijksmuseum.nl/en/rijksstudio/timeline-dutch-history/1602-trade-with-the-east-voc.

Rothwell, Donald R. "The Canadian-US Northwest Passage Dispute: A Reassessment." *Cornell International Law Journal* 26, no. 2 (1993): 331–372.

United Nations. "Agreement on Arctic Cooperation." Retrieved December 12, 2016. https://treaties.un.org/doc/publication/unts/volume%201852/volume-1852-i-31529-english.pdf.

———. "United Nations Convention on the Law of the Sea of 10 December 1982." Retrieved December 12, 2016. http://www.un.org/depts/los/convention_agreements/texts/unclos/UNCLOS-TOC.htm.

Vanderklippe, Nathan. "China Reveals Plans to Ship Cargo Across Canada's Northwest Passage." *The Globe and Mail,* April 20, 2016.

Williams, Glyn. *Arctic Labyrinth.* Berkeley and Los Angeles, CA: University of California Press, 2010.

WWF Global. "Arctic Climate Change." Retrieved December 12, 2016. http://wwf.panda.org/what_we_do/where_we_work/arctic/what_we_do/climate/.

Index

Page numbers in **boldface** are illustrations. Entries in **boldface** are glossary terms.

About the Author

Rachel Keranen is a writer from Minneapolis, Minnesota. Her work focuses on science, software, and entrepreneurship. She's passionate about learning and loves taking deep dives into science and history. In addition to the books that she writes for Cavendish Square, such as *Evolution* and *The Composition of the Universe: The Evolution of Stars and Galaxies*, Keranen's previous work includes articles in the *Minneapolis/St. Paul Business Journal* and the *London Business Matters* magazine.

Keranen enjoys traveling, biking, and spending time near water. She looks forward to traveling north of the Arctic Circle to see the Northwest Passage for herself.